Parallel History

One Period | Global Developments | Side by Side

THE MEDIEVAL
❧ WORLD ☙

500-1500

Alex Woolf

Illustrated by Victor Beuren

W
FRANKLIN WATTS
LONDON • SYDNEY

Franklin Watts
First published in Great Britain in 2017
by The Watts Publishing Group

Copyright © The Watts Publishing Group 2017

Credits
Artwork by Victor Beuren
Design: Collaborate Agency
Editor: Nicola Edwards

ISBN 978 1 4451 5738 2

Printed in China

Franklin Watts
An imprint of
Hachette Children's Group
Part of The Watts Publishing Group
Carmelite House
50 Victoria Embankment
London EC4Y 0DZ

An Hachette UK Company
www.hachette.co.uk

www.franklinwatts.co.uk

CONTENTS

✳ INTRODUCTION ✳

Historians invented the term 'medieval period' or 'Middle Ages' to describe an era in European history. It began with the fall of the Roman Empire in the late fifth century, and ended in the late fifteenth century. In this book, we are going to look at some of the developments of the medieval era – not just in Europe, but across the whole world.

Colour Key
● Africa
● Americas
● Asia
● Europe
● Australia and Oceania

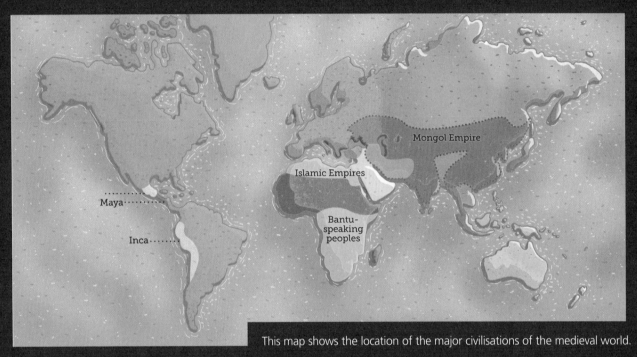

Mongol Empire

Islamic Empires

Maya

Inca

Bantu-speaking peoples

This map shows the location of the major civilisations of the medieval world.

The Church was a beacon of learning in early medieval Europe.

Europe

After the fall of the Roman Empire, the Christian Church became the most powerful institution in Europe. Civilisation went into a period of decline (the 'Dark Ages'), but from the 1000s onwards there was a revival in art and culture. Kingdoms grew more powerful, trade flourished, towns grew bigger and a class of wealthy merchants began to develop.

Islamic world

A new religion, Islam, was born in Arabia in the seventh century. It spread quickly as Muslim armies conquered the Middle East and beyond. By the eleventh century, Islamic empires controlled North Africa, southern Spain and large parts of south-western Asia.

Mansa or Emperor Musa ruled the West African Mali Empire from 1307 to 1352.

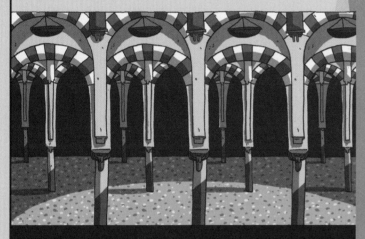

La Mezquita in Córdoba, a mosque in Moorish (Muslim) Spain.

Africa

During the medieval period, kingdoms, cities and empires arose in parts of Africa. Christianity was introduced to western Africa by Portuguese traders, while Arab traders established Islam in the north. Bantu-speaking peoples migrated from West Africa to eastern and southern regions, bringing farming and iron-working skills.

Asia

With the fall of the Gupta Empire in 550, India collapsed into warring kingdoms. Muslim conquerors arrived in the 700s, and more forcefully in the 1000s. By 1200, Islam dominated northern India. China reunited in 589, after nearly 400 years of civil war. Dynasties rose and fell until, in the 1200s, China, along with much of Central and East Asia, was conquered by the Mongols.

Li Yuan, first emperor of the Tang dynasty, China.

✳ GOVERNMENT AND SOCIETY ✳

By the Middle Ages, the democratic style of government of classical Greece and Rome had been largely forgotten. Most people were governed by tribal chiefs, monarchs or emperors. These rulers claimed their authority from God, birthright or conquest. They demanded absolute obedience from their subjects.

Islamic world

The Islamic empires of the early Middle Ages were run by caliphs (Muslim rulers). The first caliphs were chosen by the Muslim community, but it soon became a hereditary (inherited) position, dominated by powerful dynasties such as the Umayyads and Abbasids. They created large bureaucracies (administrations) to run their empires. In the later medieval period, the empires broke up into smaller emirates and sultanates. These were lands ruled by emirs and sultans.

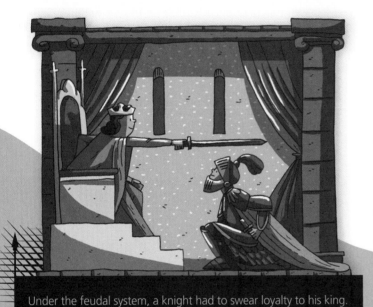

Under the feudal system, a knight had to swear loyalty to his king.

Europe

Under a system called feudalism, people offered loyalty and military service to their social superiors in exchange for land. This helped keep power in the hands of a wealthy elite, at the top of which was the king. A few societies developed a more representative type of politics. The Vikings, for example, had an assembly called the Ting where citizens could meet to accept or reject laws.

The Abbasids reached the height of their power under the caliph Harun al-Rashid.

---

661 – 750 Umayyad Caliphate	750 – 1078 Kingdom of Ghana dominates West Africa	907 – 960 Central government collapses in China

700s Feudalism emerges in Europe

750 – 1258 Abbasid Caliphate

The Sapa Inca was seen as divine – a child of the sun god.

Americas

Aztec society was strictly hierarchical. At the top was the emperor, who was advised by a council of nobles. Nobles could be warriors, priests or judges. Beneath the nobles were commoners and then slaves. Inca society had a pyramid structure, with the Sapa Inca (ruler) at the top, and below him four governors running the four quarters of the empire, helped by thousands of officials.

China

Strong leaders, including Wendi (589–604) and Taizong (626–649), created a powerful, centralised state in China. Taizong established a professional civil service (administration) and divided the country into 15 administrative regions under the control of loyal governors. This established a pattern for Chinese government under later medieval dynasties.

Kublai Khan founded the Yuan dynasty in China.

1200 – 1230 Reign of first Sapa Inca, Manco Cápac

1460s Songhai Empire becomes the most powerful West African state

1180 Kingdom of Benin is established in West Africa

Feudalism has disappeared in western Europe *1500*

c.1230 – c.1610 Mali Empire flourishes in West Africa

FOOD AND FARMING

During the Middle Ages, farming techniques and technologies continued to advance, especially in China. In Europe and Asia, manorialism was the dominant system: peasants (serfs or villeins) handed over a part of their harvest to the lord of the manor in exchange for his protection in times of danger.

Crops were harvested using sickles and scythes.

Europe

In northern Europe, open land was farmed in long strips without hedgerows. Land was left fallow about every third year to allow it to recover its fertility. Manure was used as fertiliser. Wheat, barley and oats were sown and harvested by hand. Common land was shared for grazing livestock. Southern European farmers grew wheat, olives and grapes on enclosed, square fields.

China

Chinese farmers used advanced forms of wheelbarrows, harnesses and iron ploughs. They introduced yellow ants to prey on pests that were damaging their orange trees, an early form of pest control. Under the Song dynasty (960-1279), rice replaced wheat and millet as the staple crop. In the 1200s, major terracing and irrigation projects were carried out across China.

Terraces were cut into hillsides to grow rice.

500s	Heavy plough introduced in northern Europe
900s	East African soldiers begin to eat coffee beans when they need energy for fighting

Middle Eastern merchants introduce Persian steamed or cooked rice with spices to Swahili coast in South-East Africa *c. 1000*

Indonesian settlers in Madagascar bring bananas, plantains, coconuts, sugar, yams and new kinds of rice to Africa *c. 800*

900s Wheeled ploughs used in Europe

Americas

The Maya cultivated maize, beans, tomatoes, avocados, squashes and pumpkins. In the 1400s, the Aztecs reclaimed land from the lake on which their city was built, creating *chinampas*, raised plots for growing vegetables.

The Incas grew maize, potatoes, quinoa and manioc. They built reservoirs and terraces for farming high in the Andes.

Chinampas were anchored to the lake bed and filled with manure and mud.

Islamic world

From the 700s, Muslim traders helped introduce eastern foods to the Islamic world and Europe. These included vegetables such as aubergine, spinach and chard, and spices like cumin, coriander, nutmeg and cinnamon. Arab farmers, inspired by Roman technology, irrigated their fields using water wheels, dams and reservoirs.

Arab farmers knew how to use fertilisers, fight pests and cross-fertilise crops to produce new varieties.

1200s Major irrigation schemes in China	Cassava, peanut and chili-pepper plants arrive in Central Africa from the Americas *c. 1500*
1180 Post windmill appears in France	*1300s* Colder, wetter weather in Europe causes many arable farmers to turn to sheep farming
	1400s Aztecs construct *chinampas* around their city, Tenochtitlan Incas build terraced fields in Andes

✳ ARCHITECTURE ✳

In the medieval era, people's lives were dominated by religion. Some of the most significant buildings from this period were places of worship, including Aztec pyramids, European cathedrals and ornate Hindu temples. It was also a period of almost constant warfare, and kings and nobles built sturdy fortresses for protection.

Chartres Cathedral in France, begun in 1194, is a fine example of Gothic architecture.

Angkor Wat in Cambodia, built in the 1100s, is the largest religious monument in the world.

Europe

The main form of church architecture during the 1000s–1100s was Romanesque. From the mid-1100s–1400s, Gothic architecture dominated, with thinner walls and columns, ribbed vaults and pointed arches. During the Dark Ages, most European castles were made of earth and timber. From the 1100s, architects began to build castles out of stone. Towers became round to better withstand attacks.

Asia

Islamic architecture spread through western Asia and North Africa during the Middle Ages. Features included horseshoe arches, circular domes, intricate mosaics and stonework with 'arabesque' patterns.

In China and Japan, architects built pagodas – tall, slender structures up to 15 stories high, each with an overhanging tile roof.

Americas

The Anasazi lived in what is now the south-western United States. From around 1100–1300, they built their dwellings in the sheltered recesses of cliffs, using stone, adobe or timber.

In Central America, the Aztecs built impressive temple complexes with big stepped pyramids, palaces, plazas and ball courts. The Incas in South America built temples, palaces and fortresses on mountainsides.

The Incas' most impressive creation was the city of Machu Picchu, the remains of which attract almost one million visitors every year.

The largest medieval city in sub-Saharan Africa was Great Zimbabwe. The ruins now form part of a UNESCO World Heritage Site.

Africa

Many exceptional structures were built in Africa during the medieval period. Churches were hewn out of rock in Ethiopia. The famous Great Mosque of Djenné was built in Mali in the 1200s. The Benin civilisation of West Africa produced the Walls of Benin, which extend for 16,000 km.

1250	Sun Temple at Konarch, India, built to resemble the chariot of the sun god
1260	Chartres Cathedral, among the finest examples of Gothic architecture

Machu Picchu, the remarkable Inca city perched on a mountain ridge 2.43 km above sea level **1400**

1400 Walls of Benin are built to protect the city from attack

1200s Great Mosque of Djenné built in Mali

1420 The Forbidden City built in Beijing, China

WAR AND CONFLICT

Armies became more mobile and deadly in the Middle Ages, thanks to developments such as the stirrup, gunpowder and Greek fire (an early kind of flamethrower). It was the era of the castle – providing refuge from pillaging invaders, including Vikings, Arabs, Mongols, Huns and Magyars.

The longbow was a highly effective weapon during the fourteenth and early fifteenth centuries.

Arab weapons included long swords with curved blades.

Europe

The feudal system (see page 6) led to the rise of a new class of mounted warriors, called knights, who would fight for their duke or king in exchange for land. The age of the knight lasted until the late 1400s, when countries started creating their own professional (paid) armies. From around 1000, the Church attempted to set limits to war by forbidding fighting on Sundays and during festivals, and outlawing attacks on non-combatants. Rules governed sieges, surrenders and the taking of prisoners.

Islamic world

Early Arab armies consisted of highly mobile, lightly armoured, camel-mounted fighters that scored brilliant successes against larger Byzantine and Persian armies. During the Crusades, Arab armies avoided pitched battles (where armies confront each other openly on battlefields), preferring to ambush the enemy with horse-mounted archers. The Arabs began using gunpowder during the 1200s, and were among the first to use cannons as siege machines to break through walls.

800s Gunpowder invented in China

Era of the Crusades *1096 – 1272*

First use of gunpowder on a battlefield: Song army use a firearm to capture a city in Fujian *1132*

The fire lance was one of the first gunpowder weapons.

China

During the Song dynasty, the Chinese developed gunpowder weapons such as fire lances, bombs and rockets. They expanded their army to over a million men to defend their territory against raiding armies from Central Asia. The Song also created China's first navy. When the Mongols conquered China, they introduced artillery (siege weapons) such as the trebuchet and mangonel (machines for hurling large stones or other missiles).

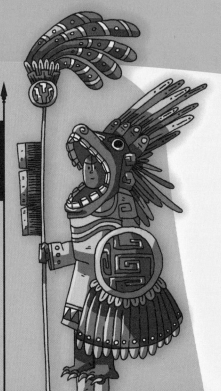

Aztec warriors wore elaborate costumes decorated with reeds and feathers.

Aztecs

The Aztecs were constantly at war. They conquered rival cities, forced them to pay tribute and took prisoners for human sacrifice. Every Aztec male was trained as a warrior from an early age. Weapons included darts, bows and arrows, slings, blowguns, maces, clubs and daggers.

SCIENCE AND TECHNOLOGY

Medieval scholars studied astronomy, mathematics, anatomy, mechanics and alchemy (an early form of chemistry). At the same time, ordinary people, such as midwives, farmers and craftspeople, advanced scientific knowledge through their daily work. In technology, there were important developments in printing, navigation, metalworking and clothmaking.

China

Paper, invented in China, spread to Japan, Korea and India in the early Middle Ages. The Chinese went on to invent woodblock printing in the seventh century, and produced the first printed book in 868. The magnetic compass, another Chinese invention, was first used for navigation in the 1040s.

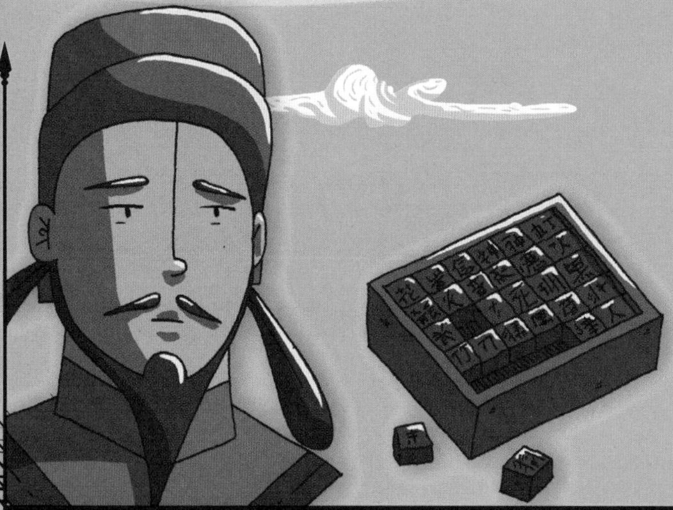

A Chinese man named Bi Sheng invented movable type printing in about 1040, 400 years before the Europeans.

Islamic world

From around 850, Arab scholars began translating and building on the knowledge of classical Greek texts. Arab chemists investigated the properties of acids and alkalis, hydrocarbons and perfumes. Al-Biruni, one of the greatest scholars of all, made important discoveries in geology, physics, mathematics, medicine and astronomy.

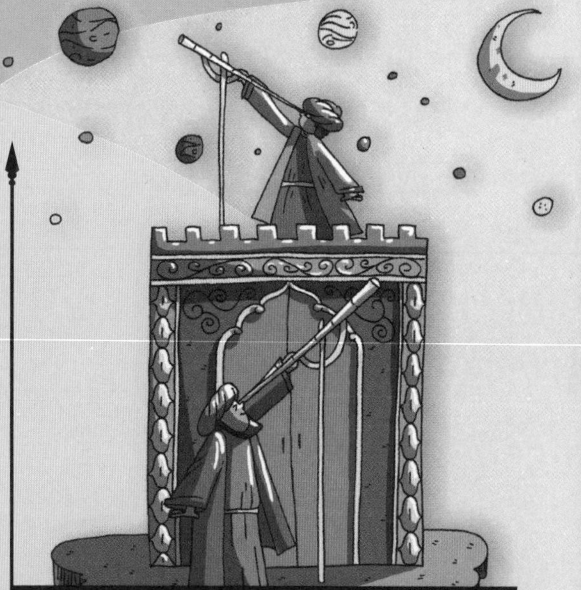

Arab astronomers mapped the stars and recorded planetary movements.

- 600s – Indian mathematicians invent negative numbers
- 751 – Paper-making skills reach the Arab world from China
- 830 – Crank reaches Europe from China
- 1000s – Horizontal loom spreads to Europe, speeding up clothmaking
- 973 – c.1052 – Life of the Muslim polymath Al-Biruni
- 1010 – English monk Eilmer of Malmesbury's glider flies 200 metres

CE 700 ... CE 800 ... CE 900 ... CE 1000 ...

India

India was an important centre of clothmaking in the Middle Ages, and the spinning wheel was invented there at some stage between the fifth and tenth centuries. The Indians were also skillful mathematicians. They developed a system of numerals that spread to the Islamic world by the ninth century, and to Europe in the tenth century.

The spinning wheel replaced the earlier method of hand spinning with a spindle.

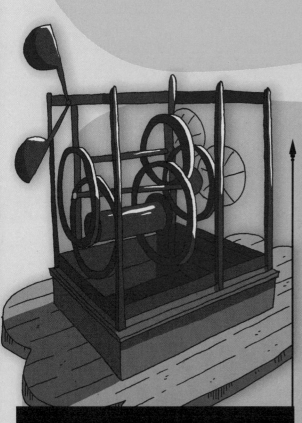

The Salisbury Clock (1386) was an early mechanical clock. It had no face, but chimed the hour.

Europe

European scientific enquiry revived in the 1200s, thanks to the founding of universities in many cities. The Italian philosopher Thomas Aquinas stressed the importance of human reason. Monks Roger Bacon of England and Germany's Albertus Magnus taught that knowledge advanced through observation. During this period, technologies invented in China began appearing in Europe, such as cast iron, the horizontal loom, paper and the crank.

 1044 Tidal mills built in Venice for grinding corn

1300s Blast furnaces start producing cast iron in Europe

 1180s First recorded use of magnetic compass in Europe (used by sailors crossing the English Channel)

 1260s Gunpowder reaches Europe from China

HEALTH AND DISEASE

For much of the Middle Ages, medicine and healing were based on ancient traditions and folklore. Physicians remained largely ignorant of the workings of the human body and the causes of illness. Diseases spread rapidly in crowded, unhygienic towns and cities. The most devastating of these was the plague, which broke out in Asia in the 1300s, and wiped out one-third of the European population.

Islamic world

Muslim scholars translated classical Greek works, and physicians made their own contributions to medical knowledge. Rhazes (c. 865–c. 930) described measles and smallpox; Ibn Sina (980–1037) wrote the *Canon of Medicine*; and Albucasis (c. 936–c. 1013) was a renowned surgeon.

Europe

From the 1000s, the ideas of the ancient Greek physicians Hippocrates and Galen began to resurface in Europe. They taught that ill health was caused by an imbalance in the four humours (bodily fluids, such as blood and phlegm). Physicians treated ailments with herbal remedies and bloodletting (the release of blood from a patient to try to cure illness). Surgeons set broken bones and closed wounds.

Albucasis treating a patient in a hospital in Córdoba, Spain.

Physicians attempted to restore the balance of humours by bloodletting.

500s Leprosy spreads from Asia to Europe

541 – 762 The first plague pandemic (when a disease spreads through a large region) in Europe

659 Su Jing publishes Xinxiu Bencao, the first Chinese herbal, listing 844 kinds of medicine

700 Japan's 'age of plagues': a series of epidemics devastates the islands

900 Islamic scholar Rhazes identifies various infectious diseases

900 The Chinese describe rickets, a disease caused by lack of vitamin D

The Aztecs knew of hundreds of different medicinal plants and herbs.

Aztecs

The Aztecs believed there were three causes of illness and injury: the displeasure of the gods; evil curses; and natural causes. Aztec physicians used a combination of prayers, spells and herbal remedies to treat patients. Their surgeons successfully treated wounds by washing them in fresh urine, applying a herb to stop the bleeding, and agave sap to promote healing.

China

Medieval Chinese physicians believed a person's health depended on the balance of yin (the female principle) and yang (the male principle) in the body. Physicians diagnosed illnesses by asking detailed questions and checking the patient's visual appearance and pulse. Cures included cold-water bathing and acupuncture.

Chinese physicians believed acupuncture (inserting needles at certain points in the body) could restore the flow of the life force (Qi).

| 1010 | Ibn Sina writes his *Canon of Medicine* | | 1400 | Leprosy has virtually disappeared from Europe |

1260s Human dissections first carried out in Bologna, Italy

1347 – 1352 The Black Death (plague) sweeps through Europe, killing one in three

ART AND LITERATURE

Most medieval art was religious in nature. Artists produced illuminated manuscripts and painted on walls and wooden panels. Sculptors created religious figures in stone, wood, bronze and ivory, or decorated temples with statues and relief carvings (carvings that stand out from a surface). Writers drew on religion, myth and folklore to create epic poems and romances.

Europe

Churches were adorned with wall paintings, painted wooden screens and stained glass windows depicting saints and scenes from the Bible. Writers increasingly abandoned Latin to write in their own languages. Famous epics included the Anglo-Saxon *Beowulf* (c. 725) and the French *Chanson de Roland* (c. 1100). Chaucer's *Canterbury Tales* was one of the first works to feature realistic, flesh-and-blood characters.

Geoffrey Chaucer, the first major poet to write in English, is buried in London's Westminster Abbey.

Islamic world

Most Islamic art took the form of decorative designs, since Islam forbids the depiction of people and animals in religious art. Copies of the holy book, the *Qur'an*, were ornamented with floral and geometric patterns, as were tiles and vases and the exteriors of mosques and palaces. Islamic literature flourished at the Abbasid court in Baghdad. The *ghazal* and the *rubā'ī* were the most popular forms of poem.

A vase with a floral decoration from early fourteenth-century Syria.

700s Manuscript illumination begins at the court of Frankish king Charlemagne

900s *The Thousand and One Nights*, a collection of fantastical adventures drawn from Indian, Persian and Arabian folk tales

800 West African potters start creating clay sculptures of their kings

800 *Hildebrandslied*, written in Old High German, tells of a battle between a father and son

India

Buddhist artists painted sacred images on temple walls and illuminated texts with colourful figures. A stunning series of paintings on cave walls in Ajanta, north-western India, tells the story of Buddha's incarnations (earthly lifetimes). Hindu sculptors decorated temples with beautifully carved figures of deities dancing and embracing.

Since 1983, the Ajanta caves with their masterpieces of Buddhist art, have been a UNESCO World Heritage Site.

Landscapes like this one were painted by Wang Ximeng in 1113.

China and Japan

In the 700s, Chinese artists began painting beautiful landscapes on silk, in shades of blue and green. Medieval Chinese poems were usually short. Like Chinese art of this period, they would suggest a mood rather than describe a scene. Some poems, called *tzu*, were sung to music. Chinese literature influenced Japanese literary works. One of the greatest of these was Murasaki Shikibu's *Tale of Genji* (c. 1010).

CHILDREN AND EDUCATION

In every medieval society, special rituals welcomed a child into the world. Muslim babies were greeted with the *shahadah* (declaration of faith) whispered into their ear. In Korea, parents hung bunches of herbs or wisps of wool on their door to announce a birth. The Incas gave a child a name and cut its hair at the age of two. In India, Hindu parents consulted an astrologer about their baby's name.

Teenage boys learning philosophy at the University of Paris in around 1300.

An Islamic scholar and his pupils.

Islamic world

Muslim baby boys were circumcised soon after birth as a sign of their faith. Education was regarded as a religious duty. Boys learned the *Qur'an* and hadith (traditions of the prophet Muhammad (PBUH)). Islamic universities, such as Al-Azhar in Egypt and Karueein in Morocco, became great centres of medieval scholarship, especially in mathematics, astronomy, geography and medicine. Education was available to Christians and Jews, as well as Muslims.

Europe

Babies were baptised a few days after birth. From age seven, boys would help their fathers and learn skills such as hunting, farming and craftwork. Girls learned housekeeping skills from their mothers. Boys from wealthy backgrounds went to school. Education was controlled by the Church, and pupils were taught by clergymen. Boys received lessons in reading, writing, Latin grammar and song.

809 — Charlemagne decrees that every cathedral and monastery in the Holy Roman Empire should found a school

859 — Karueein, the oldest university in the world, is founded in Morocco

Europe's first university is founded at Bologna 1088

Pupils at a *calmecac* being addressed by the head teacher. Punishments for disobedient Aztec children at the *calmecac* included being made to inhale smoke.

Americas

Among the Incas, only the children of nobles (people of high status) were educated. Boys studied religion, astronomy, geography, language, geometry, history, poetry and music. Girls studied housekeeping skills, spinning and weaving. Aztec noble children studied at a strict boarding school called the *calmecac*. Boys learned academic subjects and fighting; girls were taught weaving and embroidery.

In medieval China, children were taught to honour and respect their parents.

Asia

In India, both Hindu and Buddhist children attended school at their local temples. In China, Korea and Japan, the theories of the philosopher Confucius were taught in schools and colleges. Chinese students were expected to undergo a rigorous exam to qualify for a job in the civil service.

1170 University founded in Paris

1190 University founded at Oxford

1276 Some 400,000 students sit the state examination in China

1300 By this date, most European towns and cities have a grammar school

Entertainment offered relief from daily hardships during the Middle Ages. Seasonal festivals and holidays (holy days) were occasions for feasting, fairs and spectacles, including acrobats and dancing bears. At other times, people listened to music, told stories and played board and card games. Children played with dolls, balls, hoops, kites and hobbyhorses.

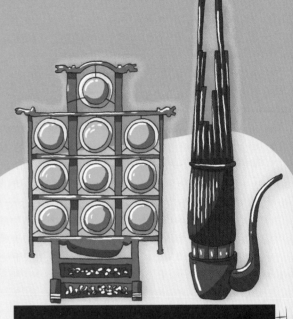

Chinese music was played on stringed instruments (*qin, zheng* and *pipa*), pipes (*sheng*) and gongs (*yunluo*).

In Europe, entertainers performed Bible stories, known as mystery plays, in front of cathedrals.

Central and East Asia

The Mongols celebrated their festivals with horse racing, archery and wrestling contests. The Chinese practised martial arts, called *wushu*. They invented card games, and the board game *weiqi*, known in Japan as *go*. In Japan, sumo wrestling became a popular spectacle, as did a form of theatre called *Noh*, performed by masked actors.

Europe

During weddings or festivals such as Mayday, peasants would dance on the village green to music from pipe and drums. The nobility went hunting or attended tournaments for their leisure. Or they might be entertained by troubadours – travelling poet-musicians playing stringed instruments such as the viol, dulcimer and lute.

500s Marionettes (stringed puppets) first appear in Constantinople

590 – 620 Chess is invented in Persia

Italian composer Guido d'Arezzo develops first system of music notation **1025**

600 Earliest known Mancala board (Mancala is an ancient African game) from Axum

700s Pipe organ first appears in Europe

Troubadours (poet-musicians) flourish in Europe **1080 – 1220**

India

The classic board games Snakes and Ladders, Ludo and Parcheesi originated in India in the sixth century. Indian music flourished under the Delhi sultanate, starting in the 1200s, when it began absorbing Arabic influences. The main stringed instrument was the *sitar* (based on the Arabic *tanbur*), accompanied by the *tabla*, a pair of tuned drums.

Americas

Native American children played games such as little sticks (like pick-up sticks); marbles, played with stones rolled along a marked board; and web weaving, a form of cat's cradle in which long fibre strings were wound into patterns. The Aztecs played a ball game called *tlachtli*, in which competing teams tried to pass a heavy ball through a stone hoop.

An Aztec dice game called *patolli*.

1200s	The tradition of griots – West African musicians and storytellers – begins in Mali
1311	First mystery plays are performed
1314	Football banned in England for being too violent
1350 – 1450	*Noh* theatre develops in Japan

CRIME AND PUNISHMENT

Crimes were punished severely in the Middle Ages. The most common punishments for serious crimes were death, usually by hanging, or mutilation – for example, chopping off a limb or branding with a hot iron. Lesser crimes were punished by whipping, or shaming offenders by making them spend a day locked in a wooden frame called the stocks.

Being put into the stocks was a common punishment for minor crimes in medieval Europe.

Europe

In the early Middle Ages, the Germanic tribes that took over the Roman Empire imposed their own law codes: if someone was murdered, the victim's family could take revenge on the killer. Those accused of crimes were subjected to 'trial by ordeal' – painful tests to indicate guilt or innocence. By the 1200s, Roman law codes had replaced Germanic ones. From this time on, states (not individuals) punished crimes, and trial was by jury.

Islamic world

For Muslims, crime was seen as an offence against Allah (God). A law code called sharia developed, based on the teachings of the Qur'an. Thieves had their hands amputated; adulterers were half buried and then stoned to death; murderers and apostates (those who renounced Islam) were beheaded with a sword.

Sometimes Muslim societies hanged criminals, as shown in this fourteenth-century Persian illustration.

529	Byzantine emperor Justinian's code of Roman law is written
600	King Ethelbert of Kent issues the oldest English law code
624	Tang law code starts to be written in China
750 – 855	Islamic law is developed by four separate schools in different parts of the Islamic world

China

During China's Tang dynasty (618–907), a law code was written that would form the basis for the laws of China, Korea, Japan and Vietnam during the Middle Ages. Ten crimes were regarded as unpardonable, including plotting rebellions, destruction of temples, tombs and imperial palaces, and disobedience to one's parents.

Prisoners in Aztec society were being kept in public in cages weighted down with stones.

Americas

In Inca society, crimes were punished ruthlessly, to serve as a warning to others. Murder, rebellion and adultery were punished with death by hanging, stoning or being pushed over a cliff. Aztec crimes included stealing another's crops and drunkenness. Punishments included strangulation and stoning. For lesser crimes, offenders might have had their homes demolished or their heads shaved.

1215   Roman Catholic Church condemns 'trial by ordeal'

1368   In China, Ming law code is written

RELIGION

Religious belief influenced every aspect of a person's life during the Middle Ages. Five religions dominated in this era: Christianity, Islam and Judaism in the West, and Buddhism and Hinduism in the East. Each religion underwent changes. There were conflicts between religions and between competing traditions within the same religion.

South Asia

In India, a new movement began within Hinduism called *bhakti*. It encouraged people to show their devotion to a particular god by singing hymns. The movement spread northwards from South India. Buddhism declined in India, but it spread to Tibet and parts of South-East Asia. By the 1200s, Islam had established itself in northern India.

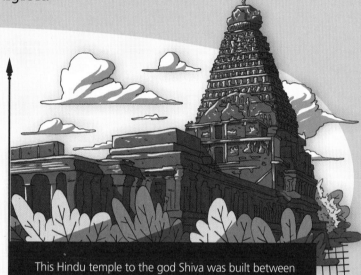

This Hindu temple to the god Shiva was built between 1004 and 1009 in Thanjavur, southern India.

Islamic world

The beliefs and rituals of Islam are based on the Qur'an, which Muslims believe was revealed to the prophet Muhammad (PBUH) by God. From the late seventh century, Islam divided into two traditions, Sunni and Shia, with differing beliefs about who should rule as caliph. Muslims lived according to a strict code known as sharia, determining their diet, clothing, prayer and social interactions. In about 900, a mystical branch of Islam developed, called Sufism.

Sufis were often called 'whirling dervishes' for their spinning dance.

---

500 St Benedict founds the Benedictine order of monks

500s Buddhism reaches Vietnam, Japan and Korea

600s Bhakti movement in Hinduism begins in South India

632 Death of the prophet Muhammad (PBUH)

900 Sufism, a mystical branch of Islam, develops

Catholic and Orthodox Churches split 1054

Pope Urban II calls Christians to go on First Crusade 1095

CE 700 ·············· CE 800 ·············· CE 900 ·············· CE 1000 ··············

Europe

Christianity was the dominant
religion of Europe and Russia,
collectively known as Christendom.
The Church was divided between
the eastern Orthodox Church,
centred in Constantinople, and the
western Catholic Church, centred in
Rome. As the western Church grew
wealthier, many of the popes who
led it became politically powerful
and corrupt.

Aztecs

The Aztecs believed in many
gods. The most important were
Tlaloc, the rain god; Tezcatlipoca,
god of destiny, war and sorcery;
and Quetzalcoatl, god of wind
and learning. They divided the
world into 13 heavens and nine
earthly layers or 'netherworlds'.
The Aztecs believed that regular
human sacrifices were needed to
keep the gods happy and the Sun
moving around the Earth.

The Aztec god Quetzalcoatl – the name
meant 'feathered serpent'.

 1200 – 1500 Muslims rule North India under the Delhi Sultanate

 1290 Jews expelled from England

1394 Jews expelled from France

DEATH AND BURIAL

Even in the most advanced societies, death at a young age was a frequent occurrence in the Middle Ages. Famine, war and outbreaks of infectious disease, along with poor diet and sanitation, led to high mortality rates. Burial rituals varied from culture to culture, depending on religious beliefs and customs.

The funeral in Konya, Turkey, of Muslim poet and mystic, Rumi (1207–1273).

Medieval European artists often portrayed death as a sinister skeleton.

Europe

Christians believed the spiritually pure went to Heaven when they died; sinners went to Hell; and those who repented their sins went to Purgatory where they paid for their misdeeds before entering Heaven. Priests would administer last rites to the dying, saying prayers and absolving them of sin. People were buried in consecrated (holy) ground, in a churchyard or crypt.

Islamic world

When a Muslim died, the body was ritually washed, clothed in white and buried before sunset on the day of death. A procession carried the body to the burial ground, and the corpse was laid on its right side facing the holy city of Mecca. Those who died fighting in the cause of Islam were believed to be guaranteed a martyr's place in Heaven.

618 – 907 During China's Tang dynasty, people are buried with pottery figurines

700s Christian burial replaces cremation in England

c.900 Vikings start burying their chieftains in *tumuli* (mounds of earth and stones)

862 Earliest known Islamic monumental tomb is built in Samarra, Iraq

CE 700 .... CE 800 .... CE 900 .... CE 1000

Tang dynasty tomb guardians from southern Gansu province, China.

China

The Chinese believed they could ease the passage of a dead person to the spirit world by providing it with useful objects. This ancient custom continued through the Middle Ages, despite the arrival of new faiths like Buddhism and Daoism. However, the nature of the objects changed. The pottery figures of the Tang dynasty were replaced by paper figures under the Song, which were ritually burned during the burial.

An Inca burial chamber in Peru's Caylloma province.

Americas

The Incas cremated or buried their dead. However, rulers were mummified and placed in tombs called *huacas*, where they were worshipped. The Aztecs buried their dead with clothing, gold, precious stones and feathers so they could live comfortably in the afterlife. Kings were buried with a dog to carry them to the netherworld. Most ordinary people were buried beneath the floors of their homes.

GLOSSARY

adobe
A kind of clay used as a building material.

arabesque
An ornamental design made up of intertwined flowing lines, found in Islamic art and architecture.

Bantu
A family of languages spoken by the Bantu peoples of central and southern Africa.

Buddhism
A religion founded by Siddartha Gautama, known as the Buddha, in North-East India in the fifth century BCE.

c.
Stands for 'circa' and means approximately or about.

cast iron
A hard alloy (a metal combining two or more elements) of iron and carbon, which can be cast in a mould.

circumcise
Cut off the foreskin of a baby boy as a religious rite.

crank
A shaft bent at right angles and used for converting reciprocating (up-down) motion to circular motion and vice versa.

Crusades
A series of military expeditions made by Europeans to recover the Holy Land from the Muslims in the 11th-13th centuries.

Daoism
A Chinese philosophy based on the teachings of Laozi, who lived in the sixth century BCE.

democratic
Describing a type of government in which the population elects representatives to pass and enact laws on their behalf.

dissection
The act of dissecting (cutting up) a body to study its internal parts.

dynasty
A line of hereditary rulers.

epidemic
A widespread outbreak of an infectious disease.

fallow
Describing farmland that has been ploughed but left for a period without being sown with crops in order to restore its fertility.

Frankish
Relating to the ancient Franks, a Germanic people who conquered Gaul (modern France) in the sixth century and controlled much of western Europe for several centuries afterwards.

ghazal
A type of poem with rhyming couplets and a repeated chorus, with each line sharing the same rhythm. Ghazals are usually about the pain of loss or separation.

Gothic (architecture)
A style characterised by pointed arches, curved vaults, large windows and ornate stonework.

hierarchical
Organised in ranks from the most powerful to the least.

Hinduism
A major religion of South Asia.

illuminated manuscript
A medieval text consisting of pages that have been decorated with gold, silver or coloured designs.

irrigation
The supply of water to farmland, usually by the digging of channels.

Islam
The religion of the Muslims, a faith believed to have been revealed through the prophet Muhammad (PBUH).

Judaism
The religions of the Jews.

jury
A body of people (typically 12 in number) sworn to give a verdict in a legal case on the basis of evidence submitted to them in court.

leprosy
A contagious disease common in the medieval world that affects the skin and nerves and in severe cases causes disfigurement and deformities.

mace
A heavy club with a spiked metal head.

martyr
A person who is killed because of their religious beliefs.

mosaic
A picture or pattern made up of small pieces of stone, tile or glass.

mosque
A Muslim place of worship.

movable type printing
A type of printing that uses movable components (e.g. individual letters and punctuation) to reproduce text, usually on paper.

polymath
A person of wide knowledge and learning.

Purgatory
A place of suffering inhabited by the souls of sinners where they make amends for their sins before entering Heaven.

reservoir
A large natural or artificial lake used as a source of water supply.

Romanesque (architecture)
A style characterised by round arches, massive vaulting, heavy columns and walls with small windows.

rubā'ī
A Persian poem, or verse of a poem, made up of four lines. The lines usually rhyme in some way, e.g. AABA or AAAA.

sanitation
Conditions relating to public health, especially access to clean drinking water and adequate sewage disposal.

smallpox
An infectious disease with symptoms including fever and pustules that leave permanent scars.

staple crop
The main or most important crop in a country or region.

stirrup
A loop with a flat base to support a horse rider's foot. They are used in pairs, attached to each side of a horse's saddle.

woodblock printing
A type of printing in which wooden blocks with designs cut into their surface are covered in ink and applied to paper.

FURTHER INFORMATION

Books

The Aztec Empire (You Choose: Historical Eras)
Elizabeth Raum and Colin MacLachlan
Raintree, 2015

Early Islamic Civilisation (Great Civilisations)
Catherine Chambers
Franklin Watts, 2016

Normans (Explore!)
Izzi Howell
Wayland, 2016

Vikings (Explore!)
Jane Bingham
Wayland, 2017

Websites

Discover life in the European Middle Ages here:
www.bbc.co.uk/education/topics/zfphvcw

Here you'll find links to pages about the culture, events, nations and people of the European Middle Ages: **www.ducksters.com/history/middle_ages_timeline.php**

Learn about the history of Islam here: **www.kidspast.com/world-history/0171-islam.php**

Find out all about Asia in the Middle Ages here: **www.kidspast.com/world-history/0232-asia-middle-ages.php**

Check out these BBC film clips about the Aztecs: **www.bbc.co.uk/education/topics/**

INDEX